Congratulations on your decision to share in and improve a child's education. **Home Learning Tools™** tablets provide a fun, educational opportunity for children to practice important school skills. Designed and developed by **Home Learning Tools** in consultation with Dr. Edward Z. Tronick, Ph.D., Harvard School of Education, Chief of the Child Development Unit at Children's Hospital, Harvard Medical School, these tablets offer a valuable learning experience you and a child can share.

The Multiplication and Division Practice Tablet will help children build confidence while mastering basic multiplication and division facts. The multiplication and division sections of the tablet are designed to begin practice with smaller numbers and build to larger numbers. The basic facts from 1x0 to 10x10 and 100÷10 to 1÷1 are included. Once children are comfortable solving the problems in the multiplication and division sections of the tablet, encourage them to try the mixed practice section that follows. There are answer pages included in the back of the tablet. Encourage children to check their own answers. SELF-CHECKING IS AN EXCELLENT LEARNING EXERCISE.

All **Home Learning Tools** educational products encourage exploration, learning, review, and practice. To enhance the child's learning experience, choose a time and place that is comfortable for both of you. Encourage the child's interest and be flexible. Children learn at different rates. Each child learns some things quickly and other things more slowly. The length of time the child spends practicing may vary from day to day. Discuss with the child the progress he or she is making. Display the finished pages for additional reinforcement and review. Encourage and reward work and improvement rather than a perfect product.

For additional review, look for other **Home Learning Tools** educational products. Congratulations on taking an active role in a child's education. Thank you for choosing **Home Learning Tools** to help.

First Published in the U.S. in 1999 by Dalmatian Press.
Copyright© 1999 Dalmatian Press.
All Rights Reserved. Printed & Bound in Canada

NOTICE: Permission for reproduction of this material by classroom teachers for classroom use only, not commercial resale, is granted by virtue of the purchase of this book.

S0-BOR-040

ABC 123 Your Letter Counts!

Home Learning Tools™ is proud to bring the highest level of quality education into your home. Please tell us about **YOURSELF** and **YOUR IDEAS** for our educational products!

You can write us at:

Home Learning Tools — P.O. Box 682068, Franklin, TN 37068-2068

Thank you and **CONGRATULATIONS** on your decision to learn the **Home Learning Tools** way.

I am most interested in teaching or learning about: _____

I like **Home Learning Tools** because: _____

I would like **Home Learning Tools** more if: _____

Name _____

Address _____

Phone _____   Age of Student _____

_____   _____
signature   date

10653a/HLT Multiplication and Division Small Tablet

Multiplication & Division Tablet

Multiplication & Division Tablet

1 x 0 = ☐

1 x 1 = ☐

1 x 2 = ☐

1 x 3 = ☐

1 x 4 = ☐

1 x 5 = ☐

1 x 6 = ☐

1 x 7 = ☐

1 x 8 = ☐

1 x 9 = ☐

1 x 10 = ☐

1 x 6 = ☐

1 x 2 = ☐

1 x 9 = ☐

1 x 4 = ☐

1 x 7 = ☐

1 x 1 = ☐

1 x 8 = ☐

1 x 3 = ☐

1 x 10 = ☐

1 x 5 = ☐

$$\begin{array}{r} 1 \\ \times\,0 \\ \hline \square \end{array} \qquad \begin{array}{r} 1 \\ \times\,8 \\ \hline \square \end{array} \qquad \begin{array}{r} 1 \\ \times\,4 \\ \hline \square \end{array}$$

$$\begin{array}{r} 1 \\ \times\,1 \\ \hline \square \end{array} \qquad \begin{array}{r} 1 \\ \times\,9 \\ \hline \square \end{array} \qquad \begin{array}{r} 1 \\ \times\,7 \\ \hline \square \end{array}$$

$$\begin{array}{r} 1 \\ \times\,2 \\ \hline \square \end{array} \qquad \begin{array}{r} 1 \\ \times\,10 \\ \hline \square \end{array} \qquad \begin{array}{r} 1 \\ \times\,9 \\ \hline \square \end{array}$$

$$\begin{array}{r} 1 \\ \times\,3 \\ \hline \square \end{array} \qquad \begin{array}{r} 1 \\ \times\,5 \\ \hline \square \end{array} \qquad \begin{array}{r} 1 \\ \times\,2 \\ \hline \square \end{array}$$

$$\begin{array}{r} 1 \\ \times\,4 \\ \hline \square \end{array} \qquad \begin{array}{r} 1 \\ \times\,1 \\ \hline \square \end{array} \qquad \begin{array}{r} 1 \\ \times\,5 \\ \hline \square \end{array}$$

$$\begin{array}{r} 1 \\ \times\,5 \\ \hline \square \end{array} \qquad \begin{array}{r} 1 \\ \times\,8 \\ \hline \square \end{array} \qquad \begin{array}{r} 1 \\ \times\,10 \\ \hline \square \end{array}$$

$$\begin{array}{r} 1 \\ \times\,6 \\ \hline \square \end{array} \qquad \begin{array}{r} 1 \\ \times\,0 \\ \hline \square \end{array} \qquad \begin{array}{r} 1 \\ \times\,4 \\ \hline \square \end{array}$$

$$\begin{array}{r} 1 \\ \times\,7 \\ \hline \square \end{array} \qquad \begin{array}{r} 1 \\ \times\,6 \\ \hline \square \end{array} \qquad \begin{array}{r} 1 \\ \times\,3 \\ \hline \square \end{array}$$

Column 1

$2 \times 0 =$ ☐

$2 \times 1 =$ ☐

$2 \times 2 =$ ☐

$2 \times 3 =$ ☐

$2 \times 4 =$ ☐

$2 \times 5 =$ ☐

$2 \times 6 =$ ☐

Column 2

$2 \times 7 =$ ☐

$2 \times 8 =$ ☐

$2 \times 9 =$ ☐

$2 \times 10 =$ ☐

$2 \times 6 =$ ☐

$2 \times 2 =$ ☐

$2 \times 9 =$ ☐

Column 3

$2 \times 4 =$ ☐

$2 \times 7 =$ ☐

$2 \times 1 =$ ☐

$2 \times 8 =$ ☐

$2 \times 3 =$ ☐

$2 \times 10 =$ ☐

$2 \times 5 =$ ☐

3

$\begin{array}{r} 2 \\ \times\ 4 \\ \hline \square \end{array}$	$\begin{array}{r} 2 \\ \times\ 8 \\ \hline \square \end{array}$	$\begin{array}{r} 2 \\ \times\ 0 \\ \hline \square \end{array}$
$\begin{array}{r} 2 \\ \times\ 7 \\ \hline \square \end{array}$	$\begin{array}{r} 2 \\ \times\ 9 \\ \hline \square \end{array}$	$\begin{array}{r} 2 \\ \times\ 1 \\ \hline \square \end{array}$
$\begin{array}{r} 2 \\ \times\ 9 \\ \hline \square \end{array}$	$\begin{array}{r} 2 \\ \times\ 10 \\ \hline \square \end{array}$	$\begin{array}{r} 2 \\ \times\ 2 \\ \hline \square \end{array}$
$\begin{array}{r} 2 \\ \times\ 2 \\ \hline \square \end{array}$	$\begin{array}{r} 2 \\ \times\ 5 \\ \hline \square \end{array}$	$\begin{array}{r} 2 \\ \times\ 3 \\ \hline \square \end{array}$
$\begin{array}{r} 2 \\ \times\ 5 \\ \hline \square \end{array}$	$\begin{array}{r} 2 \\ \times\ 1 \\ \hline \square \end{array}$	$\begin{array}{r} 2 \\ \times\ 4 \\ \hline \square \end{array}$
$\begin{array}{r} 2 \\ \times\ 10 \\ \hline \square \end{array}$	$\begin{array}{r} 2 \\ \times\ 8 \\ \hline \square \end{array}$	$\begin{array}{r} 2 \\ \times\ 5 \\ \hline \square \end{array}$
$\begin{array}{r} 2 \\ \times\ 4 \\ \hline \square \end{array}$	$\begin{array}{r} 2 \\ \times\ 0 \\ \hline \square \end{array}$	$\begin{array}{r} 2 \\ \times\ 6 \\ \hline \square \end{array}$
$\begin{array}{r} 2 \\ \times\ 3 \\ \hline \square \end{array}$	$\begin{array}{r} 2 \\ \times\ 6 \\ \hline \square \end{array}$	$\begin{array}{r} 2 \\ \times\ 7 \\ \hline \square \end{array}$

$3 \times 0 =$ ☐

$3 \times 1 =$ ☐

$3 \times 2 =$ ☐

$3 \times 3 =$ ☐

$3 \times 4 =$ ☐

$3 \times 5 =$ ☐

$3 \times 6 =$ ☐

$3 \times 7 =$ ☐

$3 \times 8 =$ ☐

$3 \times 9 =$ ☐

$3 \times 10 =$ ☐

$3 \times 6 =$ ☐

$3 \times 2 =$ ☐

$3 \times 9 =$ ☐

$3 \times 4 =$ ☐

$3 \times 7 =$ ☐

$3 \times 1 =$ ☐

$3 \times 8 =$ ☐

$3 \times 3 =$ ☐

$3 \times 10 =$ ☐

$3 \times 5 =$ ☐

$$3 \times 4 = \boxed{} \qquad 3 \times 8 = \boxed{} \qquad 3 \times 0 = \boxed{}$$

$$3 \times 7 = \boxed{} \qquad 3 \times 9 = \boxed{} \qquad 3 \times 1 = \boxed{}$$

$$3 \times 9 = \boxed{} \qquad 3 \times 10 = \boxed{} \qquad 3 \times 2 = \boxed{}$$

$$3 \times 2 = \boxed{} \qquad 3 \times 5 = \boxed{} \qquad 3 \times 3 = \boxed{}$$

$$3 \times 5 = \boxed{} \qquad 3 \times 1 = \boxed{} \qquad 3 \times 4 = \boxed{}$$

$$3 \times 10 = \boxed{} \qquad 3 \times 8 = \boxed{} \qquad 3 \times 5 = \boxed{}$$

$$3 \times 4 = \boxed{} \qquad 3 \times 0 = \boxed{} \qquad 3 \times 6 = \boxed{}$$

$$3 \times 3 = \boxed{} \qquad 3 \times 6 = \boxed{} \qquad 3 \times 7 = \boxed{}$$

$4 \times 0 =$ ☐	$4 \times 7 =$ ☐	$4 \times 4 =$ ☐
$4 \times 1 =$ ☐	$4 \times 8 =$ ☐	$4 \times 7 =$ ☐
$4 \times 2 =$ ☐	$4 \times 9 =$ ☐	$4 \times 1 =$ ☐
$4 \times 3 =$ ☐	$4 \times 10 =$ ☐	$4 \times 8 =$ ☐
$4 \times 4 =$ ☐	$4 \times 6 =$ ☐	$4 \times 3 =$ ☐
$4 \times 5 =$ ☐	$4 \times 2 =$ ☐	$4 \times 10 =$ ☐
$4 \times 6 =$ ☐	$4 \times 9 =$ ☐	$4 \times 5 =$ ☐

7

4 × 4 ☐	4 × 8 ☐	4 × 0 ☐
4 × 7 ☐	4 × 9 ☐	4 × 1 ☐
4 × 9 ☐	4 × 10 ☐	4 × 2 ☐
4 × 2 ☐	4 × 5 ☐	4 × 3 ☐
4 × 5 ☐	4 × 1 ☐	4 × 4 ☐
4 × 10 ☐	4 × 8 ☐	4 × 5 ☐
4 × 4 ☐	4 × 0 ☐	4 × 6 ☐
4 × 3 ☐	4 × 6 ☐	4 × 7 ☐

5 × 4 = ☐

5 × 7 = ☐

5 × 1 = ☐

5 × 8 = ☐

5 × 3 = ☐

5 × 10 = ☐

5 × 5 = ☐

5 × 7 = ☐

5 × 8 = ☐

5 × 9 = ☐

5 × 10 = ☐

5 × 6 = ☐

5 × 2 = ☐

5 × 9 = ☐

5 × 0 = ☐

5 × 1 = ☐

5 × 2 = ☐

5 × 3 = ☐

5 × 4 = ☐

5 × 5 = ☐

5 × 6 = ☐

9

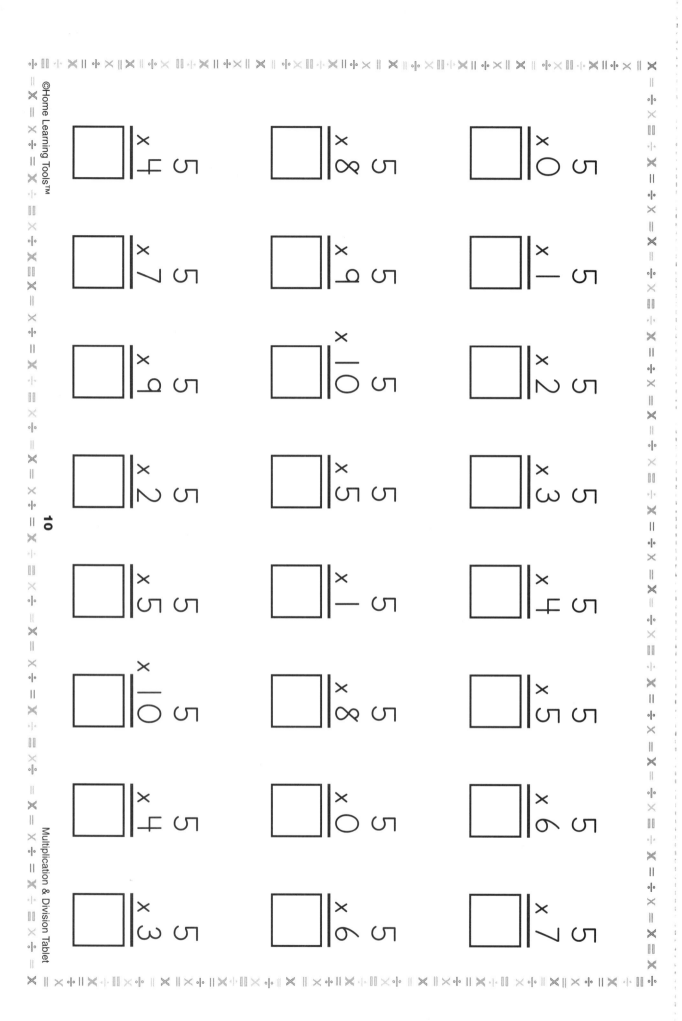

5
x0
☐

5
x1
☐

5
x2
☐

5
x3
☐

5
x4
☐

5
x5
☐

5
x6
☐

5
x7
☐

5
x8
☐

5
x9
☐

5
x10
☐

5
x5
☐

5
x1
☐

5
x8
☐

5
x0
☐

5
x6
☐

5
x4
☐

5
x7
☐

5
x9
☐

5
x2
☐

5
x5
☐

5
x10
☐

5
x4
☐

5
x3
☐

6 x 4 = □

6 x 7 = □

6 x 1 = □

6 x 8 = □

6 x 3 = □

6 x 10 = □

6 x 5 = □

6 x 7 = □

6 x 8 = □

6 x 9 = □

6 x 10 = □

6 x 6 = □

6 x 2 = □

6 x 9 = □

6 x 0 = □

6 x 1 = □

6 x 2 = □

6 x 3 = □

6 x 4 = □

6 x 5 = □

6 x 6 = □

11

12

$$6 \times 0 = \boxed{}$$

$$6 \times 1 = \boxed{}$$

$$6 \times 2 = \boxed{}$$

$$6 \times 3 = \boxed{}$$

$$6 \times 4 = \boxed{}$$

$$6 \times 5 = \boxed{}$$

$$6 \times 6 = \boxed{}$$

$$6 \times 7 = \boxed{}$$

$$6 \times 8 = \boxed{}$$

$$6 \times 9 = \boxed{}$$

$$6 \times 10 = \boxed{}$$

$$6 \times 5 = \boxed{}$$

$$6 \times 1 = \boxed{}$$

$$6 \times 8 = \boxed{}$$

$$6 \times 0 = \boxed{}$$

$$6 \times 4 = \boxed{}$$

$$6 \times 7 = \boxed{}$$

$$6 \times 9 = \boxed{}$$

$$6 \times 2 = \boxed{}$$

$$6 \times 5 = \boxed{}$$

$$6 \times 10 = \boxed{}$$

$$6 \times 4 = \boxed{}$$

$$6 \times 3 = \boxed{}$$

7 x 4 = ☐

7 x 7 = ☐

7 x 1 = ☐

7 x 8 = ☐

7 x 3 = ☐

7 x 10 = ☐

7 x 5 = ☐

7 x 7 = ☐

7 x 8 = ☐

7 x 9 = ☐

7 x 10 = ☐

7 x 6 = ☐

7 x 2 = ☐

7 x 9 = ☐

7 x 0 = ☐

7 x 1 = ☐

7 x 2 = ☐

7 x 3 = ☐

7 x 4 = ☐

7 x 5 = ☐

7 x 6 = ☐

$$\begin{array}{r} 7 \\ \times\,0 \\ \hline \square \end{array} \qquad \begin{array}{r} 7 \\ \times\,8 \\ \hline \square \end{array} \qquad \begin{array}{r} 7 \\ \times\,4 \\ \hline \square \end{array}$$

$$\begin{array}{r} 7 \\ \times\,1 \\ \hline \square \end{array} \qquad \begin{array}{r} 7 \\ \times\,9 \\ \hline \square \end{array} \qquad \begin{array}{r} 7 \\ \times\,7 \\ \hline \square \end{array}$$

$$\begin{array}{r} 7 \\ \times\,2 \\ \hline \square \end{array} \qquad \begin{array}{r} 7 \\ \times\,10 \\ \hline \square \end{array} \qquad \begin{array}{r} 7 \\ \times\,9 \\ \hline \square \end{array}$$

$$\begin{array}{r} 7 \\ \times\,3 \\ \hline \square \end{array} \qquad \begin{array}{r} 7 \\ \times\,5 \\ \hline \square \end{array} \qquad \begin{array}{r} 7 \\ \times\,2 \\ \hline \square \end{array}$$

$$\begin{array}{r} 7 \\ \times\,4 \\ \hline \square \end{array} \qquad \begin{array}{r} 7 \\ \times\,1 \\ \hline \square \end{array} \qquad \begin{array}{r} 7 \\ \times\,5 \\ \hline \square \end{array}$$

$$\begin{array}{r} 7 \\ \times\,5 \\ \hline \square \end{array} \qquad \begin{array}{r} 7 \\ \times\,8 \\ \hline \square \end{array} \qquad \begin{array}{r} 7 \\ \times\,10 \\ \hline \square \end{array}$$

$$\begin{array}{r} 7 \\ \times\,6 \\ \hline \square \end{array} \qquad \begin{array}{r} 7 \\ \times\,0 \\ \hline \square \end{array} \qquad \begin{array}{r} 7 \\ \times\,4 \\ \hline \square \end{array}$$

$$\begin{array}{r} 7 \\ \times\,7 \\ \hline \square \end{array} \qquad \begin{array}{r} 7 \\ \times\,6 \\ \hline \square \end{array} \qquad \begin{array}{r} 7 \\ \times\,3 \\ \hline \square \end{array}$$

8 x 0 = ☐
8 x 1 = ☐
8 x 2 = ☐
8 x 3 = ☐
8 x 4 = ☐
8 x 5 = ☐
8 x 6 = ☐

8 x 7 = ☐
8 x 8 = ☐
8 x 9 = ☐
8 x 10 = ☐
8 x 6 = ☐
8 x 2 = ☐
8 x 9 = ☐

8 x 4 = ☐
8 x 7 = ☐
8 x 1 = ☐
8 x 8 = ☐
8 x 3 = ☐
8 x 10 = ☐
8 x 5 = ☐

Multiplication & Division Tablet

©Home Learning Tools™

8	8	8
× 0	× 8	× 4
8	8	8
× 1	× 9	× 7
8	8	8
× 2	× 10	× 9
8	8	8
× 3	× 5	× 2
8	8	8
× 4	× 1	× 5
8	8	8
× 5	× 8	× 10
8	8	8
× 6	× 0	× 4
8	8	8
× 7	× 6	× 3

9 x 0 = ☐   9 x 7 = ☐   9 x 4 = ☐

9 x 1 = ☐   9 x 8 = ☐   9 x 7 = ☐

9 x 2 = ☐   9 x 9 = ☐   9 x 1 = ☐

9 x 3 = ☐   9 x 10 = ☐   9 x 8 = ☐

9 x 4 = ☐   9 x 6 = ☐   9 x 3 = ☐

9 x 5 = ☐   9 x 2 = ☐   9 x 10 = ☐

9 x 6 = ☐   9 x 9 = ☐   9 x 5 = ☐

Multiplication & Division Tablet

$$9 \times 0 = \square \qquad 9 \times 8 = \square \qquad 9 \times 4 = \square$$

$$9 \times 1 = \square \qquad 9 \times 9 = \square \qquad 9 \times 7 = \square$$

$$9 \times 2 = \square \qquad 9 \times 10 = \square \qquad 9 \times 9 = \square$$

$$9 \times 3 = \square \qquad 9 \times 5 = \square \qquad 9 \times 2 = \square$$

$$9 \times 4 = \square \qquad 9 \times 1 = \square \qquad 9 \times 5 = \square$$

$$9 \times 5 = \square \qquad 9 \times 8 = \square \qquad 9 \times 10 = \square$$

$$9 \times 6 = \square \qquad 9 \times 0 = \square \qquad 9 \times 4 = \square$$

$$9 \times 7 = \square \qquad 9 \times 6 = \square \qquad 9 \times 3 = \square$$

10 × 4 = ☐

10 × 7 = ☐

10 × 1 = ☐

10 × 8 = ☐

10 × 3 = ☐

10 × 10 = ☐

10 × 5 = ☐

10 × 7 = ☐

10 × 8 = ☐

10 × 9 = ☐

10 × 10 = ☐

10 × 6 = ☐

10 × 2 = ☐

10 × 9 = ☐

10 × 0 = ☐

10 × 1 = ☐

10 × 2 = ☐

10 × 3 = ☐

10 × 4 = ☐

10 × 5 = ☐

10 × 6 = ☐

19

$10 \times 0 = \square$	$10 \times 8 = \square$	$10 \times 4 = \square$
$10 \times 1 = \square$	$10 \times 9 = \square$	$10 \times 7 = \square$
$10 \times 2 = \square$	$10 \times 10 = \square$	$10 \times 9 = \square$
$10 \times 3 = \square$	$10 \times 5 = \square$	$10 \times 2 = \square$
$10 \times 4 = \square$	$10 \times 1 = \square$	$10 \times 5 = \square$
$10 \times 5 = \square$	$10 \times 8 = \square$	$10 \times 10 = \square$
$10 \times 6 = \square$	$10 \times 0 = \square$	$10 \times 4 = \square$
$10 \times 7 = \square$	$10 \times 6 = \square$	$10 \times 3 = \square$

8 x 1 = ☐

3 x 3 = ☐

10 x 7 = ☐

1 x 4 = ☐

3 x 8 = ☐

7 x 4 = ☐

5 x 5 = ☐

8 x 7 = ☐

7 x 0 = ☐

2 x 5 = ☐

4 x 3 = ☐

1 x 9 = ☐

2 x 6 = ☐

5 x 6 = ☐

5 x 9 = ☐

3 x 1 = ☐

2 x 2 = ☐

5 x 7 = ☐

10 x 6 = ☐

3 x 4 = ☐

6 x 6 = ☐

21

3 × 2	4 × 1	10 × 4
8 × 5	10 × 8	0 × 7
5 × 7	6 × 2	4 × 9
9 × 8	2 × 5	6 × 2
1 × 4	7 × 1	5 × 5
7 × 9	3 × 8	2 × 10
0 × 6	9 × 0	4 × 4
3 × 10	1 × 6	8 × 3

8 x 3 = ☐

7 x 7 = ☐

10 x 6 = ☐

1 x 3 = ☐

3 x 7 = ☐

1 x 4 = ☐

9 x 9 = ☐

8 x 6 = ☐

7 x 5 = ☐

2 x 8 = ☐

4 x 2 = ☐

1 x 9 = ☐

2 x 6 = ☐

5 x 5 = ☐

5 x 7 = ☐

3 x 4 = ☐

2 x 0 = ☐

5 x 8 = ☐

10 x 7 = ☐

3 x 1 = ☐

6 x 2 = ☐

23

$$\begin{array}{r} 3 \\ \times 3 \\ \hline \square \end{array} \qquad \begin{array}{r} 4 \\ \times 5 \\ \hline \square \end{array} \qquad \begin{array}{r} 6 \\ \times 7 \\ \hline \square \end{array} \qquad \begin{array}{r} 1 \\ \times 8 \\ \hline \square \end{array} \qquad \begin{array}{r} 2 \\ \times 4 \\ \hline \square \end{array} \qquad \begin{array}{r} 8 \\ \times 9 \\ \hline \square \end{array} \qquad \begin{array}{r} 5 \\ \times 6 \\ \hline \square \end{array} \qquad \begin{array}{r} 9 \\ \times 10 \\ \hline \square \end{array}$$

$$\begin{array}{r} 9 \\ \times 1 \\ \hline \square \end{array} \qquad \begin{array}{r} 7 \\ \times 8 \\ \hline \square \end{array} \qquad \begin{array}{r} 10 \\ \times 2 \\ \hline \square \end{array} \qquad \begin{array}{r} 4 \\ \times 5 \\ \hline \square \end{array} \qquad \begin{array}{r} 9 \\ \times 7 \\ \hline \square \end{array} \qquad \begin{array}{r} 6 \\ \times 8 \\ \hline \square \end{array} \qquad \begin{array}{r} 1 \\ \times 0 \\ \hline \square \end{array} \qquad \begin{array}{r} 3 \\ \times 6 \\ \hline \square \end{array}$$

$$\begin{array}{r} 5 \\ \times 4 \\ \hline \square \end{array} \qquad \begin{array}{r} 6 \\ \times 7 \\ \hline \square \end{array} \qquad \begin{array}{r} 2 \\ \times 9 \\ \hline \square \end{array} \qquad \begin{array}{r} 8 \\ \times 2 \\ \hline \square \end{array} \qquad \begin{array}{r} 7 \\ \times 5 \\ \hline \square \end{array} \qquad \begin{array}{r} 3 \\ \times 10 \\ \hline \square \end{array} \qquad \begin{array}{r} 1 \\ \times 4 \\ \hline \square \end{array} \qquad \begin{array}{r} 10 \\ \times 3 \\ \hline \square \end{array}$$

Multiplication & Division Tablet

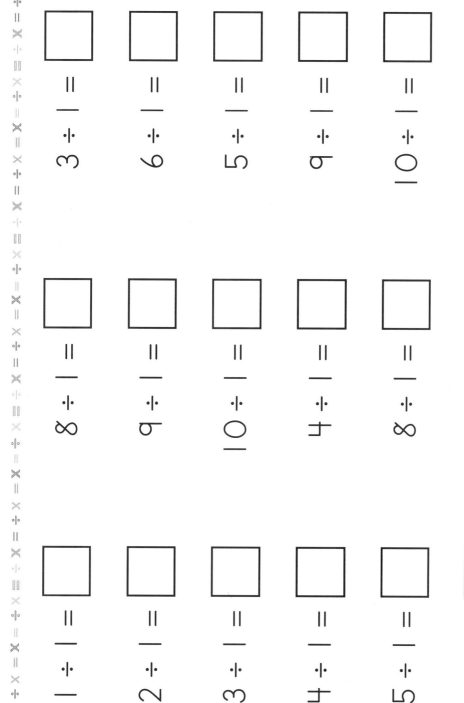
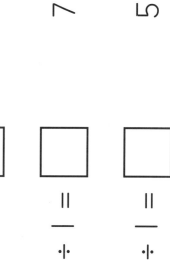

3 ÷ 1 = ☐

6 ÷ 1 = ☐

5 ÷ 1 = ☐

9 ÷ 1 = ☐

10 ÷ 1 = ☐

7 ÷ 1 = ☐

5 ÷ 1 = ☐

8 ÷ 1 = ☐

9 ÷ 1 = ☐

10 ÷ 1 = ☐

4 ÷ 1 = ☐

8 ÷ 1 = ☐

2 ÷ 1 = ☐

1 ÷ 1 = ☐

1 ÷ 1 = ☐

2 ÷ 1 = ☐

3 ÷ 1 = ☐

4 ÷ 1 = ☐

5 ÷ 1 = ☐

6 ÷ 1 = ☐

7 ÷ 1 = ☐

25

Problem	Problem	Problem	Problem
1 × 3 = ☐	1 × 6 = ☐	1 × 8 = ☐	1 × 1 = ☐
1 × 7 = ☐	1 × 2 = ☐	1 × 4 = ☐	1 × 5 = ☐
1 × 6 = ☐	1 × 7 = ☐	1 × 8 = ☐	1 × 9 = ☐
1 × 1 = ☐	1 × 2 = ☐	1 × 3 = ☐	1 × 4 = ☐
		1 × 10 = ☐	1 × 10 = ☐

$18 \div 2 = $ ☐

$2 \div 2 = $ ☐

$20 \div 2 = $ ☐

$8 \div 2 = $ ☐

$12 \div 2 = $ ☐

$16 \div 2 = $ ☐

$8 \div 2 = $ ☐

$16 \div 2 = $ ☐

$18 \div 2 = $ ☐

$20 \div 2 = $ ☐

$10 \div 2 = $ ☐

$14 \div 2 = $ ☐

$6 \div 2 = $ ☐

$4 \div 2 = $ ☐

$2 \div 2 = $ ☐

$4 \div 2 = $ ☐

$6 \div 2 = $ ☐

$8 \div 2 = $ ☐

$10 \div 2 = $ ☐

$12 \div 2 = $ ☐

$14 \div 2 = $ ☐

27

$2\,\overline{)2}\ \square$

$2\,\overline{)12}\ \square$

$2\,\overline{)8}\ \square$

$2\,\overline{)14}\ \square$

$2\,\overline{)4}\ \square$

$2\,\overline{)14}\ \square$

$2\,\overline{)18}\ \square$

$2\,\overline{)16}\ \square$

$2\,\overline{)6}\ \square$

$2\,\overline{)16}\ \square$

$2\,\overline{)6}\ \square$

$2\,\overline{)6}\ \square$

$2\,\overline{)10}\ \square$

$2\,\overline{)8}\ \square$

$2\,\overline{)18}\ \square$

$2\,\overline{)4}\ \square$

$2\,\overline{)2}\ \square$

$2\,\overline{)6}\ \square$

$2\,\overline{)20}\ \square$

$2\,\overline{)10}\ \square$

$2\,\overline{)20}\ \square$

$21 \div 3 =$ ☐

$12 \div 3 =$ ☐

$24 \div 3 =$ ☐

$30 \div 3 =$ ☐

$18 \div 3 =$ ☐

$9 \div 3 =$ ☐

$12 \div 3 =$ ☐

$24 \div 3 =$ ☐

$27 \div 3 =$ ☐

$30 \div 3 =$ ☐

$15 \div 3 =$ ☐

$6 \div 3 =$ ☐

$18 \div 3 =$ ☐

$3 \div 3 =$ ☐

$3 \div 3 =$ ☐

$6 \div 3 =$ ☐

$9 \div 3 =$ ☐

$12 \div 3 =$ ☐

$15 \div 3 =$ ☐

$18 \div 3 =$ ☐

$21 \div 3 =$ ☐

29

30

$$3 \overline{\smash{)}3} \;\square$$

$$3 \overline{\smash{)}6} \;\square$$

$$3 \overline{\smash{)}9} \;\square$$

$$3 \overline{\smash{)}12} \;\square$$

$$3 \overline{\smash{)}12} \;\square$$

$$3 \overline{\smash{)}9} \;\square$$

$$3 \overline{\smash{)}24} \;\square$$

$$3 \overline{\smash{)}27} \;\square$$

$$3 \overline{\smash{)}18} \;\square$$

$$3 \overline{\smash{)}21} \;\square$$

$$3 \overline{\smash{)}24} \;\square$$

$$3 \overline{\smash{)}30} \;\square$$

$$3 \overline{\smash{)}12} \;\square$$

$$3 \overline{\smash{)}15} \;\square$$

$$3 \overline{\smash{)}18} \;\square$$

$$3 \overline{\smash{)}27} \;\square$$

$$3 \overline{\smash{)}9} \;\square$$

$$3 \overline{\smash{)}15} \;\square$$

$$3 \overline{\smash{)}3} \;\square$$

$$3 \overline{\smash{)}30} \;\square$$

$4 \div 4 = \square$	$32 \div 4 = \square$	$12 \div 4 = \square$
$8 \div 4 = \square$	$36 \div 4 = \square$	$24 \div 4 = \square$
$12 \div 4 = \square$	$40 \div 4 = \square$	$40 \div 4 = \square$
$16 \div 4 = \square$	$16 \div 4 = \square$	$28 \div 4 = \square$
$20 \div 4 = \square$	$20 \div 4 = \square$	$4 \div 4 = \square$
$24 \div 4 = \square$	$8 \div 4 = \square$	$36 \div 4 = \square$
$28 \div 4 = \square$	$40 \div 4 = \square$	$32 \div 4 = \square$

Multiplication & Division Tablet

$$4\overline{)4}\ \boxed{} \qquad 4\overline{)8}\ \boxed{} \qquad 4\overline{)12}\ \boxed{} \qquad 4\overline{)16}\ \boxed{} \qquad 4\overline{)20}\ \boxed{}$$

$$4\overline{)24}\ \boxed{} \qquad 4\overline{)28}\ \boxed{} \qquad 4\overline{)32}\ \boxed{} \qquad 4\overline{)36}\ \boxed{} \qquad 4\overline{)40}\ \boxed{}$$

$$4\overline{)40}\ \boxed{} \qquad 4\overline{)16}\ \boxed{} \qquad 4\overline{)4}\ \boxed{} \qquad 4\overline{)8}\ \boxed{} \qquad 4\overline{)32}\ \boxed{}$$

$$4\overline{)28}\ \boxed{} \qquad 4\overline{)24}\ \boxed{} \qquad 4\overline{)36}\ \boxed{} \qquad 4\overline{)20}\ \boxed{} \qquad 4\overline{)12}\ \boxed{}$$

$40 \div 5 =$ ☐

$5 \div 5 =$ ☐

$35 \div 5 =$ ☐

$45 \div 5 =$ ☐

$15 \div 5 =$ ☐

$40 \div 5 =$ ☐

$30 \div 5 =$ ☐

$40 \div 5 =$ ☐

$45 \div 5 =$ ☐

$50 \div 5 =$ ☐

$20 \div 5 =$ ☐

$50 \div 5 =$ ☐

$10 \div 5 =$ ☐

$25 \div 5 =$ ☐

$5 \div 5 =$ ☐

$10 \div 5 =$ ☐

$15 \div 5 =$ ☐

$20 \div 5 =$ ☐

$25 \div 5 =$ ☐

$30 \div 5 =$ ☐

$35 \div 5 =$ ☐

33

5 | 5 ☐   5 | 10 ☐   5 | 15 ☐   5 | 25 ☐

5 | 30 ☐   5 | 35 ☐   5 | 30 ☐   5 | 40 ☐

5 | 15 ☐   5 | 40 ☐   5 | 35 ☐   5 | 45 ☐

5 | 20 ☐   5 | 45 ☐   5 | 5 ☐   5 | 20 ☐

5 | 25 ☐   5 | 50 ☐   5 | 50 ☐

34

$6 \div 6 =$ □ $48 \div 6 =$ □ $24 \div 6 =$ □

$12 \div 6 =$ □ $54 \div 6 =$ □ $18 \div 6 =$ □

$18 \div 6 =$ □ $60 \div 6 =$ □ $54 \div 6 =$ □

$24 \div 6 =$ □ $18 \div 6 =$ □ $12 \div 6 =$ □

$30 \div 6 =$ □ $30 \div 6 =$ □ $42 \div 6 =$ □

$36 \div 6 =$ □ $48 \div 6 =$ □ $6 \div 6 =$ □

$42 \div 6 =$ □ $36 \div 6 =$ □ $60 \div 6 =$ □

Multiplication & Division Tablet

$$6\,\overline{)6}\quad\square$$

$$6\,\overline{)36}\quad\square$$

$$6\,\overline{)24}\quad\square$$

$$6\,\overline{)54}\quad\square$$

$$6\,\overline{)12}\quad\square$$

$$6\,\overline{)42}\quad\square$$

$$6\,\overline{)36}\quad\square$$

$$6\,\overline{)48}\quad\square$$

$$6\,\overline{)18}\quad\square$$

$$6\,\overline{)48}\quad\square$$

$$6\,\overline{)42}\quad\square$$

$$6\,\overline{)18}\quad\square$$

$$6\,\overline{)24}\quad\square$$

$$6\,\overline{)54}\quad\square$$

$$6\,\overline{)6}\quad\square$$

$$6\,\overline{)12}\quad\square$$

$$6\,\overline{)30}\quad\square$$

$$6\,\overline{)60}\quad\square$$

$$6\,\overline{)60}\quad\square$$

$$6\,\overline{)30}\quad\square$$

$21 \div 7 =$ ☐

$42 \div 7 =$ ☐

$35 \div 7 =$ ☐

$63 \div 7 =$ ☐

$70 \div 7 =$ ☐

$49 \div 7 =$ ☐

$35 \div 7 =$ ☐

$56 \div 7 =$ ☐

$63 \div 7 =$ ☐

$70 \div 7 =$ ☐

$28 \div 7 =$ ☐

$56 \div 7 =$ ☐

$14 \div 7 =$ ☐

$7 \div 7 =$ ☐

$7 \div 7 =$ ☐

$14 \div 7 =$ ☐

$21 \div 7 =$ ☐

$28 \div 7 =$ ☐

$35 \div 7 =$ ☐

$42 \div 7 =$ ☐

$49 \div 7 =$ ☐

$7 \overline{)7}$

$7 \overline{)14}$

$7 \overline{)21}$

$7 \overline{)28}$

$7 \overline{)35}$

$7 \overline{)42}$

$7 \overline{)49}$

$7 \overline{)56}$

$7 \overline{)63}$

$7 \overline{)70}$

$7 \overline{)28}$

$7 \overline{)42}$

$7 \overline{)49}$

$7 \overline{)7}$

$7 \overline{)63}$

$7 \overline{)70}$

$7 \overline{)21}$

$7 \overline{)56}$

$7 \overline{)14}$

$7 \overline{)35}$

©Home Learning Tools™

$8 \div 8 =$ ☐	$64 \div 8 =$ ☐	$40 \div 8 =$ ☐
$16 \div 8 =$ ☐	$72 \div 8 =$ ☐	$16 \div 8 =$ ☐
$24 \div 8 =$ ☐	$80 \div 8 =$ ☐	$40 \div 8 =$ ☐
$32 \div 8 =$ ☐	$72 \div 8 =$ ☐	$32 \div 8 =$ ☐
$40 \div 8 =$ ☐	$64 \div 8 =$ ☐	$80 \div 8 =$ ☐
$48 \div 8 =$ ☐	$48 \div 8 =$ ☐	$56 \div 8 =$ ☐
$56 \div 8 =$ ☐	$8 \div 8 =$ ☐	$24 \div 8 =$ ☐

40

$8\overline{)8}$ $8\overline{)16}$ $8\overline{)24}$ $8\overline{)32}$ $8\overline{)40}$

$8\overline{)48}$ $8\overline{)56}$ $8\overline{)64}$ $8\overline{)72}$ $8\overline{)80}$

$8\overline{)24}$ $8\overline{)48}$ $8\overline{)56}$ $8\overline{)8}$ $8\overline{)72}$

$8\overline{)32}$ $8\overline{)64}$ $8\overline{)80}$ $8\overline{)16}$ $8\overline{)40}$

$9 \div 9 =$ ☐	$72 \div 9 =$ ☐	$18 \div 9 =$ ☐
$18 \div 9 =$ ☐	$81 \div 9 =$ ☐	$54 \div 9 =$ ☐
$27 \div 9 =$ ☐	$90 \div 9 =$ ☐	$90 \div 9 =$ ☐
$36 \div 9 =$ ☐	$45 \div 9 =$ ☐	$81 \div 9 =$ ☐
$45 \div 9 =$ ☐	$72 \div 9 =$ ☐	$45 \div 9 =$ ☐
$54 \div 9 =$ ☐	$18 \div 9 =$ ☐	$63 \div 9 =$ ☐
$63 \div 9 =$ ☐	$27 \div 9 =$ ☐	$36 \div 9 =$ ☐

41

$9\overline{)9}$ $9\overline{)18}$ $9\overline{)27}$ $9\overline{)36}$ $9\overline{)45}$

$9\overline{)54}$ $9\overline{)63}$ $9\overline{)72}$ $9\overline{)81}$ $9\overline{)90}$

$9\overline{)18}$ $9\overline{)27}$ $9\overline{)9}$

$9\overline{)54}$ $9\overline{)63}$ $9\overline{)72}$ $9\overline{)81}$ $9\overline{)90}$

$9\overline{)27}$ $9\overline{)36}$ $9\overline{)45}$

30 ÷ 10 =	☐
60 ÷ 10 =	☐
50 ÷ 10 =	☐
90 ÷ 10 =	☐
100 ÷ 10 =	☐
70 ÷ 10 =	☐
50 ÷ 10 =	☐

80 ÷ 10 =	☐
90 ÷ 10 =	☐
100 ÷ 10 =	☐
40 ÷ 10 =	☐
80 ÷ 10 =	☐
20 ÷ 10 =	☐
10 ÷ 10 =	☐

10 ÷ 10 =	☐
20 ÷ 10 =	☐
30 ÷ 10 =	☐
40 ÷ 10 =	☐
50 ÷ 10 =	☐
60 ÷ 10 =	☐
70 ÷ 10 =	☐

$10\overline{)10}$ ☐ $10\overline{)80}$ ☐ $10\overline{)30}$ ☐ $10\overline{)90}$ ☐ $10\overline{)50}$ ☐

$10\overline{)20}$ ☐ $10\overline{)60}$ ☐ $10\overline{)70}$ ☐ $10\overline{)40}$ ☐ $10\overline{)100}$ ☐

$10\overline{)60}$ ☐ $10\overline{)70}$ ☐ $10\overline{)80}$ ☐ $10\overline{)90}$ ☐ $10\overline{)100}$ ☐

$10\overline{)10}$ ☐ $10\overline{)20}$ ☐ $10\overline{)30}$ ☐ $10\overline{)40}$ ☐ $10\overline{)50}$ ☐

$24 \div 6 =$ ☐

$24 \div 8 =$ ☐

$18 \div 9 =$ ☐

$35 \div 7 =$ ☐

$21 \div 3 =$ ☐

$12 \div 2 =$ ☐

$40 \div 4 =$ ☐

$81 \div 9 =$ ☐

$5 \div 5 =$ ☐

$72 \div 9 =$ ☐

$40 \div 4 =$ ☐

$18 \div 9 =$ ☐

$8 \div 1 =$ ☐

$36 \div 9 =$ ☐

$2 \div 1 =$ ☐

$21 \div 3 =$ ☐

$70 \div 7 =$ ☐

$36 \div 6 =$ ☐

$2 \div 2 =$ ☐

$72 \div 8 =$ ☐

$15 \div 5 =$ ☐

$2\overline{)12}$ $8\overline{)24}$ $9\overline{)27}$ $7\overline{)14}$ $3\overline{)18}$

$6\overline{)42}$ $5\overline{)25}$ $1\overline{)1}$ $10\overline{)80}$ $4\overline{)40}$

$10\overline{)50}$ $3\overline{)6}$ $7\overline{)21}$ $1\overline{)9}$ $8\overline{)8}$

$9\overline{)63}$ $6\overline{)48}$ $2\overline{)20}$ $4\overline{)12}$ $5\overline{)20}$

Multiplication & Division Tablet

$12 \div 4 =$ ☐	$35 \div 7 =$ ☐	$6 \div 3 =$ ☐
$20 \div 2 =$ ☐	$21 \div 3 =$ ☐	$60 \div 10 =$ ☐
$8 \div 8 =$ ☐	$24 \div 6 =$ ☐	$28 \div 4 =$ ☐
$30 \div 5 =$ ☐	$45 \div 9 =$ ☐	$18 \div 2 =$ ☐
$81 \div 9 =$ ☐	$8 \div 1 =$ ☐	$25 \div 5 =$ ☐
$2 \div 1 =$ ☐	$14 \div 7 =$ ☐	$63 \div 9 =$ ☐
$80 \div 10 =$ ☐	$24 \div 8 =$ ☐	$16 \div 4 =$ ☐

$2\overline{)6}$ ☐

$5\overline{)25}$ ☐

$4\overline{)24}$ ☐

$1\overline{)4}$ ☐

$6\overline{)54}$ ☐

$9\overline{)63}$ ☐

$2\overline{)12}$ ☐

$3\overline{)6}$ ☐

$10\overline{)80}$ ☐

$7\overline{)7}$ ☐

$1\overline{)10}$ ☐

$7\overline{)49}$ ☐

$3\overline{)15}$ ☐

$9\overline{)63}$ ☐

$2\overline{)8}$ ☐

$10\overline{)20}$ ☐

$6\overline{)48}$ ☐

$1\overline{)1}$ ☐

$4\overline{)12}$ ☐

$5\overline{)35}$ ☐

$6 \times 4 =$ ☐

$1 \times 6 =$ ☐

$21 \div 3 =$ ☐

$24 \div 6 =$ ☐

$28 \div 4 =$ ☐

$3 \times 9 =$ ☐

$7 \times 2 =$ ☐

$35 \div 7 =$ ☐

$8 \times 3 =$ ☐

$20 \div 4 =$ ☐

$25 \div 5 =$ ☐

$7 \times 6 =$ ☐

$24 \div 8 =$ ☐

$4 \times 3 =$ ☐

$14 \div 7 =$ ☐

$8 \times 7 =$ ☐

$36 \div 6 =$ ☐

$72 \div 9 =$ ☐

$16 \div 4 =$ ☐

$36 \div 6 =$ ☐

$1 \times 0 =$ ☐

49

40 ÷ 8 = ☐   27 ÷ 9 = ☐   6 ÷ 3 = ☐

8 x 4 = ☐   8 x 0 = ☐   5 x 4 = ☐

35 ÷ 5 = ☐   20 ÷ 2 = ☐   50 ÷ 5 = ☐

3 x 7 = ☐   28 ÷ 4 = ☐   4 x 6 = ☐

16 ÷ 2 = ☐   7 x 4 = ☐   16 ÷ 4 = ☐

3 x 5 = ☐   24 ÷ 6 = ☐   9 x 9 = ☐

1 x 9 = ☐   4 x 8 = ☐   2 x 2 = ☐

$2 \div 2 =$ ☐ $42 \div 7 =$ ☐ $1 \times 5 =$ ☐

$9 \div 3 =$ ☐ $18 \div 3 =$ ☐ $14 \div 7 =$ ☐

$8 \times 2 =$ ☐ $8 \times 3 =$ ☐ $8 \times 8 =$ ☐

$3 \times 5 =$ ☐ $10 \div 2 =$ ☐ $2 \times 9 =$ ☐

$12 \div 6 =$ ☐ $4 \times 8 =$ ☐ $30 \div 6 =$ ☐

$45 \div 9 =$ ☐ $63 \div 7 =$ ☐ $6 \times 3 =$ ☐

$1 \times 8 =$ ☐ $30 \div 5 =$ ☐ $4 \times 4 =$ ☐

Multiplication & Division Tablet

8 x 6 = ☐

54 ÷ 6 = ☐

3 x 7 = ☐

7 x 6 = ☐

12 ÷ 2 = ☐

16 ÷ 8 = ☐

9 x 7 = ☐

32 ÷ 8 = ☐

2 x 10 = ☐

18 ÷ 9 = ☐

40 ÷ 5 = ☐

3 x 7 = ☐

6 x 3 = ☐

16 ÷ 8 = ☐

12 ÷ 4 = ☐

8 x 1 = ☐

48 ÷ 6 = ☐

5 x 5 = ☐

40 ÷ 10 = ☐

6 x 6 = ☐

50 ÷ 5 = ☐

Multiplication & Division Tablet

$5 \times 6 =$ ☐

$36 \div 6 =$ ☐

$7 \times 7 =$ ☐

$3 \times 6 =$ ☐

$16 \div 2 =$ ☐

$8 \div 8 =$ ☐

$2 \times 7 =$ ☐

$16 \div 8 =$ ☐

$4 \times 10 =$ ☐

$81 \div 9 =$ ☐

$45 \div 5 =$ ☐

$8 \times 7 =$ ☐

$3 \times 3 =$ ☐

$64 \div 8 =$ ☐

$12 \div 4 =$ ☐

$7 \times 0 =$ ☐

$36 \div 6 =$ ☐

$10 \times 5 =$ ☐

$42 \div 7 =$ ☐

$5 \times 6 =$ ☐

$10 \div 5 =$ ☐

10 × 10 = ☐

5 × 7 = ☐   4 × 4 = ☐   1 × 7 = ☐

42 ÷ 7 = ☐

3 × 7 = ☐   9 ÷ 9 = ☐

15 ÷ 5 = ☐   25 ÷ 5 = ☐   6 × 5 = ☐

8 ÷ 1 = ☐   4 × 3 = ☐   49 ÷ 7 = ☐

2 × 1 = ☐   5 × 8 = ☐   9 × 8 = ☐

72 ÷ 8 = ☐   5 ÷ 5 = ☐

16 ÷ 4 = ☐

40 ÷ 4 = ☐

54 ÷ 6 = ☐

54

Multiplication & Division Tablet

Answer Page

Page 1

1×0=0 1×7=7 1×4=4
1×1=1 1×8=8 1×7=7
1×2=2 1×9=9 1×1=1
1×3=3 1×10=10 1×8=8
1×4=4 1×6=6 1×3=3
1×5=5 1×2=2 1×10=10
1×6=6 1×9=9 1×5=5

Page 2

1×7=7 1×6=6 1×3=3
1×5=5 1×0=0 1×4=4
1×4=4 1×1=1 1×5=5
1×3=3 1×5=5 1×2=2
1×2=2 1×10=10 1×9=9
1×1=1 1×9=9 1×7=7
1×0=0 1×8=8 1×4=4

Page 3

2×0=0 2×7=14 2×4=8
2×1=2 2×8=16 2×7=14
2×2=4 2×9=18 2×1=2
2×3=6 2×10=20 2×8=16
2×4=8 2×6=12 2×3=6
2×5=10 2×2=4 2×10=20
2×6=12 2×9=18 2×5=10

Page 4

2×7=14 2×6=12 2×3=6
2×5=10 2×0=0 2×4=8
2×4=8 2×1=2 2×5=10
2×3=6 2×5=10 2×2=4
2×2=4 2×10=20 2×9=18
2×1=2 2×9=18 2×7=14
2×0=0 2×8=16 2×4=8

Page 5

3×0=0 3×4=12 3×7=21
3×1=3 3×7=21 3×8=24
3×2=6 3×1=3 3×9=27
3×3=9 3×8=24 3×10=30
3×4=12 3×3=9 3×6=18
3×5=15 3×10=30 3×2=6
3×6=18 3×5=15 3×9=27

Page 6

3×7=21 3×6=18 3×3=9
3×5=15 3×0=0 3×4=12
3×4=12 3×1=3 3×5=15
3×3=9 3×5=15 3×2=6
3×2=6 3×10=30 3×9=27
3×1=3 3×9=27 3×7=21
3×0=0 3×8=24 3×4=12

Page 7

4×0=0 4×4=16 4×7=28
4×1=4 4×7=28 4×8=32
4×2=8 4×1=4 4×9=36
4×3=12 4×8=32 4×10=40
4×4=16 4×3=12 4×6=24
4×5=20 4×10=40 4×2=8
4×6=24 4×5=20 4×9=36

Page 8

4×7=28 4×6=24 4×3=12
4×5=20 4×0=0 4×4=16
4×4=16 4×1=4 4×5=20
4×3=12 4×5=20 4×2=8
4×2=8 4×10=40 4×9=36
4×1=4 4×9=36 4×7=28
4×0=0 4×8=32 4×4=16

Page 9

5×0=0 5×7=35 5×4=20
5×1=5 5×8=40 5×7=35
5×2=10 5×9=45 5×1=5
5×3=15 5×10=50 5×8=40
5×4=20 5×6=30 5×3=15
5×5=25 5×2=10 5×10=50
5×6=30 5×9=45 5×5=25

Multiplication & Division Tablet

Answer Page

Page 10

(5× boxed answers)
0, 5, 10, 15, 20, 25, 5, 20, 40, 25, 30, 35, 35, 50, 10, 25, 50, 15, 45, 45, 35, 40, 20, 30, 40, 50, 10, 15

Page 11

6×0=0
6×1=6
6×2=12
6×3=18
6×4=24
6×5=30
6×6=36
6×7=42
6×8=48
6×9=54
6×10=60

6×4=24
6×7=42
6×1=6
6×8=48
6×6=36
6×2=12
6×3=18
6×8=48
6×1=6
6×7=42
6×10=60
6×3=18
6×5=30

Page 12

8×0=0
8×1=8
8×2=16
8×3=24
8×4=32
8×5=40
8×6=48
8×7=56
8×8=64
8×9=72
8×10=80

8×4=32
8×7=56
8×8=64
8×3=24
8×1=8
8×10=80
8×5=40

(6× boxed answers)
0, 6, 12, 24, 48, 54, 54, 60, 42, 30, 18, 24, 12, 30, 6, 24, 36, 48, 60, 42, 18, 36, 42, 18

Page 13

7×0=0
7×1=7
7×2=14
7×3=21
7×4=28
7×5=35
7×6=42
7×7=49
7×8=56
7×9=63
7×10=70

7×4=28
7×7=49
7×1=7
7×8=56
7×6=42
7×2=14
7×10=70
7×3=21
7×8=56
7×1=7
7×7=49
7×5=35

Page 14

(7× boxed answers)
0, 7, 14, 21, 28, 35, 7, 49, 63, 56, 49, 63, 28, 14, 35, 7, 70, 56, 42, 0, 21

Page 15

8×0=0
8×1=8
8×2=16
8×3=24
8×4=32
8×5=40
8×6=48

8×7=56
8×8=64
8×6=48
8×10=80
8×2=16
8×3=24
8×8=64
8×1=8
8×9=72

Page 16

(8× boxed answers)
0, 8, 16, 32, 64, 72, 80, 16, 40, 24, 8, 40, 80, 64, 32, 24, 56, 72, 72, 48, 56

Page 17

9×0=0
9×1=9
9×2=18
9×3=27
9×4=36
9×5=45
9×6=54

9×7=63
9×8=72
9×6=54
9×10=90
9×9=81
9×2=18
9×8=72
9×1=9
9×7=63
9×4=36
9×3=27
9×10=90
9×5=45

Page 18

(9× boxed answers)
0, 9, 18, 36, 72, 81, 81, 90, 63, 45, 27, 18, 9, 45, 90, 54, 36, 72, 54, 63, 27

©Home Learning Tools™

Multiplication & Division Tablet

Answer Page

Page 19
10x0=0   10x4=40
10x1=10   10x7=70
10x2=20   10x8=80
10x3=30   10x9=90
10x4=40   10x10=100
10x5=50   10x6=60
10x6=60   10x3=30
             10x2=20
             10x10=100
             10x9=90

Page 20
(vertical multiplication problems)

10×1=10, 10×2=20, 10×3=30, 10×4=40, 10×5=50, 10×6=60, 10×7=70
10×8=80, 10×9=90, 10×10=100, 10×1=10, 10×5=50, 10×2=20, 10×4=40
10×9=90, 10×6=60, 10×5=50, 10×8=80, 10×10=100, 10×9=90, 10×3=30
10×8=80, 10×4=40, 10×7=70, 10×6=60, 10×3=30

Page 21
5x9=45   8x7=56   8x1=8
3x1=3   7x0=0   3x3=9
2x2=4   2x5=10   10x7=70
5x7=35   4x3=12   1x4=4
10x6=60 1x9=9   3x8=24
3x4=12   2x6=12   7x4=28
6x6=36   5x6=30   5x5=25

Page 22
(vertical multiplication problems)

2×3=6, 8×5=40, 5×7=35, 0×6=0, 7×9=63, 3×10=30
4×1=4, 10×8=80, 9×8=72, 9×0=0, 3×8=24, 1×6=6
10×4=40, 0×7=0, 7×1=7, 5×5=25, 4×4=16, 8×3=24
             6×2=12, 5×10=20, 6×6=36, 4×9=36

Page 23
5x7=35   8x6=48   8x3=24
3x4=12   7x5=35   7x7=49
2x0=0   2x8=16   10x6=60
5x8=40   4x2=8   1x3=3
10x7=70 1x9=9   3x7=21
3x1=3   2x6=12   1x4=4
6x2=12   5x5=25   9x9=81

Page 24
(vertical multiplication problems)

3×3=9, 6×7=42, 4×5=20, 8×9=72, 5×6=30, 9×10=90
9×1=9, 10×2=20, 4×5=20, 6×8=48, 3×6=18
5×4=20, 2×7=14, 8×2=16, 7×5=35, 1×4=4
             9×7=63, 10×3=30, 10×3=30

Page 25
1÷1=1   8÷1=8   3÷1=3
2÷1=2   9÷1=9   6÷1=6
3÷1=3   10÷1=10 5÷1=5
4÷1=4   4÷1=4   9÷1=9
5÷1=5   8÷1=8   10÷1=10
6÷1=6   2÷1=2   7÷1=7
7÷1=7   1÷1=1   5÷1=5

Page 26
(division problems)

1)1=1, 2)2=1, 3)3=1, 4)4=1, 5)5=1
6)6=1, 7)7=1, 8)8=1, 4)4=1, 5)5=1
7)7=1, 2)2=1, 4)4=1, 5)5=1, 10)10=1
3)3=1, 6)6=1, 8)8=1, 10)10=1, 9)9=1

Page 27
2÷2=1   16÷2=8 18÷2=9
4÷2=2   18÷2=9 2÷2=1
6÷2=3   20÷2=10 20÷2=10
8÷2=4   10÷2=5 8÷2=4
10÷2=5 14÷2=7 12÷2=6
12÷2=6 6÷2=3   16÷2=8
14÷2=7 4÷2=2   8÷2=4

©Home Learning Tools™   Multiplication & Division Tablet

Page 28

quotient	division
1	2)2
6	2)12
2	2)4
8	2)16
2	2)4
9	2)18
2	2)14
7	2)14
8	2)16
3	2)6
1	2)2
2	2)24
3	2)6
2	2)18
2	2)6
2	2)2
4	2)8
3	2)6
9	2)18
2	2)24
5	2)20
5	2)10
10	2)20

Page 29

3÷3=1	24÷3=8	21÷3=7
6÷3=2	27÷3=9	12÷3=4
12÷3=4	30÷3=10	24÷3=8
9÷3=3	15÷3=5	30÷3=10
15÷3=5	6÷3=2	18÷3=6
18÷3=6	18÷3=6	9÷3=3
21÷3=7	3÷3=1	12÷3=4
	12÷3=4	

Page 30 (÷3)

quotient	division
1	3)3
2	3)6
3	3)9
4	3)12
6	3)18
8	3)24
5	3)15
7	3)21
10	3)30
9	3)27

Page 31

4÷4=1	32÷4=8	12÷4=3
8÷4=2	36÷4=9	24÷4=6
12÷4=3	40÷4=10	40÷4=10
16÷4=4	16÷4=4	28÷4=7
20÷4=5	40÷4=10	4÷4=1
24÷4=6	8÷4=2	36÷4=9
28÷4=7	20÷4=5	32÷4=8

Page 32 (÷4)

quotient	division
1	4)4
2	4)8
3	4)12
4	4)16
6	4)24
7	4)28
8	4)32
9	4)36
10	4)40
5	4)20

Page 33

5÷5=1	40÷5=8	15÷5=3
10÷5=2	45÷5=9	30÷5=6
15÷5=3	50÷5=10	50÷5=10
20÷5=4	20÷5=4	35÷5=7
25÷5=5	50÷5=10	25÷5=5
30÷5=6	10÷5=2	40÷5=8
35÷5=7	45÷5=9	30÷5=6

Page 34 (÷5)

quotient	division
1	5)5
6	5)30
2	5)10
3	5)15
2	5)10
7	5)35
8	5)40
6	5)30
9	5)45
7	5)35
4	5)20
5	5)25
1	5)50
9	5)45
50	

Page 35

6÷6=1	48÷6=8	24÷6=4
12÷6=2	54÷6=9	18÷6=3
18÷6=3	60÷6=10	54÷6=9
24÷6=4	18÷6=3	12÷6=2
30÷6=5	30÷6=5	6÷6=1
36÷6=6	48÷6=8	42÷6=7
42÷6=7	36÷6=6	60÷6=10

Page 36 (÷6)

quotient	division
1	6)6
2	6)12
3	6)18
4	6)24
6	6)36
7	6)42
8	6)48
10	6)60
9	6)54
5	6)30

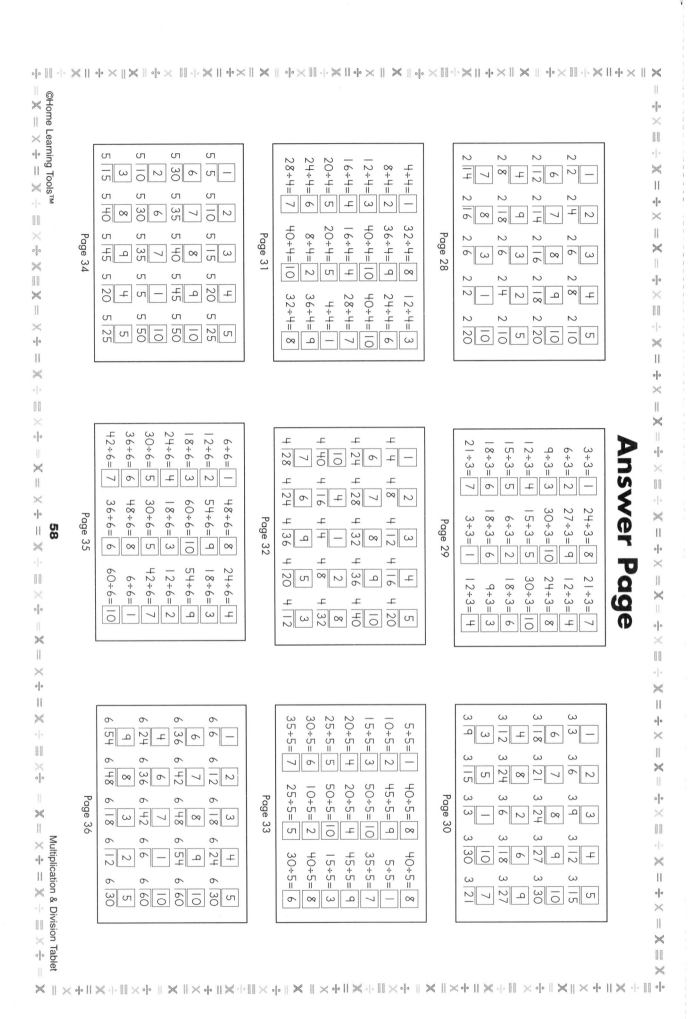

©Home Learning Tools™

Multiplication & Division Tablet

Answer Page

Page 37

7÷7= 1	56÷7= 8	21÷7= 3
14÷7= 2	63÷7= 9	42÷7= 6
21÷7= 3	70÷7= 10	35÷7= 5
28÷7= 4	28÷7= 4	63÷7= 9
35÷7= 5	56÷7= 8	70÷7= 10
42÷7= 6	14÷7= 2	49÷7= 7
49÷7= 7	7÷7= 1	35÷7= 5

Page 38

7)7 = 1	7)14 = 2	7)21 = 3
7)42 = 6	7)49 = 7	7)28 = 4
7)14 = 2	7)56 = 8	7)63 = 9
7)28 = 4	7)49 = 7	7)63 = 9
7)21 = 3	7)42 = 6	7)14 = 2
	7)8 = ...	7)7 = 1
	7)56 = 8	7)56 = 8

Page 39

8÷8= 1	64÷8= 8	40÷8= 5
16÷8= 2	72÷8= 9	16÷8= 2
24÷8= 3	80÷8= 10	40÷8= 5
32÷8= 4	72÷8= 9	32÷8= 4
40÷8= 5	64÷8= 8	80÷8= 10
48÷8= 6	48÷8= 6	56÷8= 7
56÷8= 7	8÷8= 1	24÷8= 3

Page 40

8)8 = 1	8)24 = 3	8)32 = 4
8)16 = 2	8)64 = 8	8)72 = 9
8)48 = 6	8)56 = 7	8)80 = 10
8)24 = 3	8)48 = 6	8)8 = ...
8)32 = 4	8)64 = 8	8)16 = 2
	8)56 = 7	8)72 = 9
	8)80 = 10	8)40 = 5

Page 41

9÷9= 1	72÷9= 8	18÷9= 2
18÷9= 2	81÷9= 9	54÷9= 6
27÷9= 3	90÷9= 10	90÷9= 10
36÷9= 4	45÷9= 5	81÷9= 9
45÷9= 5	72÷9= 8	45÷9= 5
54÷9= 6	18÷9= 2	63÷9= 7
63÷9= 7	27÷9= 3	36÷9= 4

Page 42

9)9 = 1	9)18 = 2	9)45 = 5
9)54 = 6	9)27 = 3	9)36 = 4
9)18 = 2	9)63 = 7	9)90 = 10
9)63 = 7	9)72 = 8	9)81 = 9
9)54 = 6	9)81 = 9	9)81 = 9
9)18 = 2	9)90 = 10	9)36 = 4
9)27 = 3		9)45 = 5

Page 43

10÷10= 1	80÷10= 8	30÷10= 3
20÷10= 2	90÷10= 9	60÷10= 6
30÷10= 3	100÷10= 10	50÷10= 5
40÷10= 4	40÷10= 4	90÷10= 9
50÷10= 5	80÷10= 8	100÷10= 10
60÷10= 6	20÷10= 2	70÷10= 7
70÷10= 7	10÷10= 1	50÷10= 5

Page 44

10)10 = 1	10)20 = 2	10)50 = 5
10)60 = 6	10)30 = 3	10)40 = 4
10)20 = 2	10)40 = 4	10)100 = 10
10)80 = 8	10)60 = 6	10)90 = 9
10)10 = 1	10)80 = 8	10)100 = 10
	10)70 = 7	10)30 = 3
		10)50 = 5

Page 45

24÷6= 4	81÷9= 9	2÷1= 2
24÷8= 3	5÷5= 1	21÷3= 7
18÷9= 2	72÷9= 8	70÷7= 10
35÷7= 5	40÷4= 10	36÷6= 6
21÷3= 7	18÷9= 2	2÷2= 1
12÷2= 6	8÷1= 8	72÷8= 9
40÷4= 10	36÷9= 4	15÷5= 3

Multiplication & Division Tablet

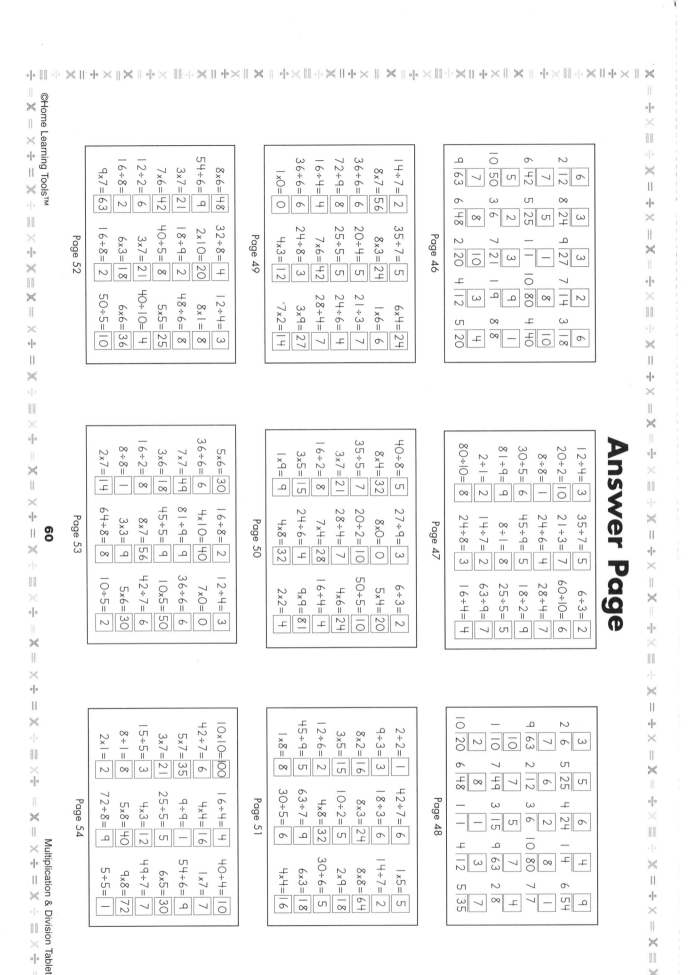

Answer Page